This Book Belongs To:

_____

About Us

Brissa Ocean is an independent brand, that offers a world of creativity and artistic expression through a wide range of unique and captivating drawings.

Our books are designed to provide you with an opportunity to disconnect, find tranquility, and rediscover the joy of creation.

Head on over to our Amazon Store for more:

Thanks for adding a bit more color to the world!

Brissa Ocean

A look at the inside content

OCELOT

Navigate life's complexities with agility and grace. Be self-reliant, adaptable, and let your inner resilience light your path in the darkest of times.

GIRAFFE

Stretch towards your dreams; stand tall in your uniqueness and reach high, for the best leaves are found at the top of the tallest trees.

PEACOCK

Embrace the brilliance within you, spreading your vibrant spirit for all to see, and inspiring others with your display of confidence and splendor.

OKAPI

Stride through life's journey with quiet curiosity, blending beautifully into your surroundings while maintaining your unique path.

EAGLE

Soar with a majestic spirit, embracing the freedom of the skies, while keeping a keen eye on the opportunities that lie ahead.

BONGO

Move through life with unique elegance, confidently embracing your individuality, and leaving a trail of beauty in your quiet, purposeful steps.

FOX

Navigate life with cunning and adaptability, blending grace with resilience, and always staying one step ahead in your journey.

COUGAR

Embody grace and power in solitude, mastering the art of independence, while remaining vigilant and courageous in the face of adversity.

ALPACA

Tread softly yet with great impact, bringing warmth and gentleness to your interactions, a beacon of calm in a bustling world

ANDEAN COCK OF THE ROCK

Stand out with your bold, vibrant presence, embracing life with fearless enthusiasm and a striking charm that turns every challenge into an opportunity to shine.

MOOSE

Walk through life's hurdles with assuredness and elegance, utilizing your inner fortitude and presence to journey along the roads less ventured.

COW

Approach life with a gentle and nurturing spirit. Stay grounded in your values, and find contentment in the simple, tranquil moments.

PANDA BEAR

Walk through life with a gentle footprint. Seek harmony, indulge in life's simple joys, and find strength in quiet moments of solitude and reflection.

CHEETAH

Dash through challenges with unmatched speed and focus. Keep your eyes on the goal, embrace your nimbleness, and remember that the quickest way forward isn't always a straight line

RACCOON

Be resourceful and adaptable, finding clever solutions in unexpected places, and never underestimate the value of curiosity and playfulness

HIPPOPOTAMUS

Navigate life's waters with robust determination, embodying strength and resilience, making your presence known in the vast currents of existence.

ZEBRA

Live boldly and unapologetically. Celebrate your individuality, stand strong in solidarity, and maintain your uniqueness in a world of conformity.

BALD EAGLE

Soar above life's trials with keen insight and majestic grace, embodying the spirit of freedom and a perspective that sees beyond the ordinary.

BABIRUSA

Move through life with a unique stride, embracing your individuality and the unconventional path, undeterred by life's twists and turns.

KOALA

Navigate life's branches with serene calmness, embracing a slower pace that allows you to savor each moment and find joy in the small things.

CAPYBARA

Navigate your journey with calm assurance,
finding strength in serenity and harmony,
while adapting effortlessly to life's ever-
changing currents

LEMUR

Dance through life's challenges with a playful heart, adaptable and light, creating a symphony of joy and connection in the world around you.

RHINOCEROS

Walk through life with a gentle footprint.
Seek harmony, indulge in life's simple joys,
and find strength in quiet moments of
solitude and reflection.

GERENUK

Reach for the uncommon, stretching beyond the ordinary with grace and persistence, finding nourishment in the rare and overlooked

LION

Lead your domain with courage and a noble heart. Protect and cherish those you care for, and let your voice be heard, echoing the strength of your convictions.

LLAMA

Carry your burdens with steadfast calm and gentle dignity, navigating life's ups and downs with a peaceful, enduring spirit

MANED WOLF

Embrace life with a fierce spirit and a gentle heart, striking a balance between independence and the need for connection.

JAGUAR

Move through life with the stealth and beauty of a shadow in the moonlight, powerful and graceful, master of your own journey

HORSE

Carry yourself with strength and elegance.
Run towards your dreams with
determination, letting the winds of
perseverance guide you forward.

TAKIN

Stand tall and unique, unafraid to show your true colors, thriving in even the most unexpected of environments.

QUOKKA

Face the world with a smile, radiating
positivity and joy, and finding happiness in
the simplest of life's pleasures.

BEAR

Embrace the strength within you, nurturing and protecting, while also finding solace in life's quiet, introspective moments

TAPIR

Navigate life with a gentle tenacity, moving steadily through challenges, rooted in a deep understanding of the world around you.

TENREC

Embrace the little things in life, finding strength in your uniqueness and forging a path that's vibrantly your own.

ELEPHANT

Move through life with a gentle, yet powerful presence, remembering that true strength lies in unity, compassion, and intelligence.

ARMADILLO

Navigate life's challenges with a hardy resilience, protecting your inner self while adapting to the changing landscapes around you.

HYENA

Find humor amidst challenges, forge deep connections within your community, and harness the strength of perseverance and thoughtful strategy.

KANGAROO

Leap through life's obstacles with boundless energy and a nurturing spirit, always moving forward with strength and familial devotion.

POLAR BEAR

Find strength in the quiet of the frozen landscapes, standing steadfast and formidable against the severest of nature's challenges.

KOMODO DRAGON

Walk with confidence and tenacity, a fearless explorer in life's rugged terrain, commanding respect through your presence and determination.

KINKAJU

Explore life with joyful curiosity, agile and adaptable, finding delight in the smallest details and the hidden corners of the world.

LANGUR

Leap through life with wisdom and grace, your eyes shining with understanding, a harmonious bridge between the earth and the sky.

SNOW LEOPARD

Move through life with silent grace and resilience, thriving in solitude and showing strength in the face of the harshest elements.

SLOTH

Move through life at your own pace, finding wisdom in stillness and the power in taking time to just be.

OSTRICH

Stride confidently across life's vast landscapes, standing out with your unique stride, and viewing the world from a perspective all your own

OWL

See the world from a higher perspective, using wisdom and insight to navigate the darkness, and soar gracefully above life's challenges.

MEERKAT

Stay vigilant and community-oriented,
facing the world with curiosity and
teamwork, finding strength in unity and the
joy of shared experiences

SQUIRREL

Navigate life's twists and turns with agility and grace, storing up rich experiences and memories like precious treasures.

FOSSA

Embrace the mystery within you, navigating life with agility and cunning, always finding your way through the complexities with subtle grace.

MARKHOR

Climb the mountains of life with determination and strength, standing majestically against life's challenges, a symbol of resilience and beauty.

TIGER

Stride with confidence and power. Be fearless and assertive, understanding that your presence alone can command respect and attention.

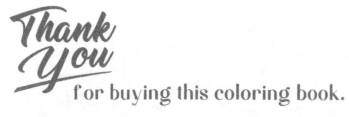 

Thank You

for buying this coloring book.

If you enjoyed your journey through these images, please consider taking a few minutes to leave a review.

It would mean the world to me, and I believe it can also help others find enjoyment in these pages.

This QR code will direct you to the Amazon reviews section.

Thanks for adding a bit more color to the world!

Brissa Ocean

Made in the USA
Coppell, TX
20 December 2024

42496631R00059